Made in United States
Troutdale, OR
05/29/2025

31749720R00070